NO LONGER PROPERTY OF
ANYTHINK LIBRARIES/
RANGEVIEW LIBRARY DISTRICT

# César

*¡Sí, se puede!*

Yes, We Can!

Carmen T. Bernier-Grand

Illustrated by David Diaz

**two lions**

**two lions**

To those who "not only champion *La Raza* but
*la raza humana*," as César did.
May the readers of this book get to know what the heart of a champion
is, so that they may recognize the champion in
themselves and learn to look for the champions in their lives.

—C.B-G.

For Kerri Ann Pratschner—
"Ren, you know I'm lost without you."

—D.D.

## ACKNOWLEDGMENTS

Thanks to Margery Cuyler, my editor, for encouraging me while this book evolved
and changed shape in the quiet of the Sterling Room for Writers at the Multnomah
County Library.

*Mil gracias* to those mentioned above but also to my first readers: authors
Pamela Smith Hill, Gretchen Olson, and Winifred Morris; growers Eugene Euwer
and Phil Olson; educators Hope Crandall and Dr. Miguel López; illustrators
Carolyn Conahan and David Diaz; my *mejicanitos* Celedonio Montes, José Romero,
Gloria Rodríguez, and Esteban Campos; and the people at the Cesar E. Chavez
Foundation—Juan-Carlos Orellana, Ankush Agawal, and Julie C. Rodríguez; and
to my friend, Kay Winters, without whom this book would not have happened.

Thanks to the Cesar E. Chavez Foundation for evaluating the text.

Text copyright © 2004 by Carmen T. Bernier-Grand
Illustrations copyright © 2004 by David Diaz

All rights reserved
Amazon Publishing,
Attn: Amazon Children's Publishing,
P.O. Box 400818,
Las Vegas, NV 89140
www.amazon.com/amazonchildrenspublishing

Library of Congress Cataloging-in-Publication Data
Bernier-Grand, Carmen T.
César : sí, se puede! = yes, we can! / Carmen T. Bernier-Grand ; illustrated by David Diaz.
p. cm.
Includes bibliographical references.
ISBN: 978-0-7614-5833-3 (paperback)
1. Chavez, Cesar, 1927—Juvenile poetry. 2. Mexican American migrant agricultural laborers—Juvenile poetry.
3. Migrant agricultural laborers—Juvenile poetry. 4. Mexican Americans—Juvenile poetry. 5. Labor leaders—
Juvenile poetry. 6. Children's poetry, American. [1. Chavez, Cesar, 1927—Poetry. 2. Labor leaders—Poetry. 3.
Mexican Americans—Poetry. 4. Migrant labor—Poetry. 5. American poetry.] I. Diaz, David, ill. II. Title.

PS3602.E7624C47 2004
811'.54—dc22
2003026866

The illustrations were rendered in Photoshop.
Book design by Patrice Sheridan
Editor: Margery Cuyler
Printed in China

# Contents

# Who Could Tell?

*¡Híjole!*
Who could tell?

Who could tell
that Cesario Estrada Chávez,
the shy American
wearing a checkered shirt,
walking with a cane to ease his back
from the burden of the fields,
could organize so many people
to march for *La Causa,* The Cause?

Who could tell
that he with a soft *pan dulce* voice,
hair the color of mesquite,
and downcast, Aztec eyes,
would have the courage to speak up
for the *campesinos*
to get better pay,
better housing,
better health?

*¡Híjole!*
Who could tell?

# Cesario

Cesario was his real name.
Not See-zar. Not even César.

Cesario Estrada Chávez
was the name given to him
by his parents,
Juana Estrada
and
Librado Chávez
*en el día de su santo,*
March 31, 1927,
near Yuma, Arizona.

Cesario,
named for his *abuelito,*
better known as Papá Chayo.

Calling him See-zar Cha-VEZ
came later,
when his teacher couldn't
or wouldn't
call him Cesario.

People called him
See-zar Cha-VEZ
or César Chávez.
It was better to call him
Friend of the Farm Workers,
for these were *la gente*
for whom he struggled.

# Dad: Librado Chávez

Large
*como un guitarrón.*
Nearly six feet tall.
Huge, strong hands.
Quiet.
Taught César
how to make cars
out of sardine cans
and tractors
out of spools of thread.
"Never afraid of work
and often did too much."
Found it dishonorable
to be fired for being lazy.
"But if somebody was fired
for standing up for a person's rights,
it was quite honorable."
Tugged at César's ears
and patted his head.

# Mom: Juana Estrada

Tiny
*como una vihuela.*
Little more than five feet.
Small hands—long thin fingers.
Talked a lot.
"Her tongue skipping,
as fast as her mind."
Often spoke to César in *dichos,*
taught him from the Bible.
"What does the Lord require of you,
but to do justice,
to love kindness,
and to walk humbly with your God?"
Hated violence.
"God gave you senses,
like your eyes, and mind, and tongue
and you can get out of everything."
Gave César *manzanilla* tea,
and hugged him tight.

# Happy Moments

"I had more happy moments
as a child than unhappy moments."

At the foot of a hot,
rocky hill in the desert
near Yuma, Arizona,
Librado and Papá Chayo
built an adobe home.

It had two wings
divided by a covered breezeway.
"There was an endless droning
of flies around it,
a sound that seemed to always be there
and to have been there always."

10

The Chávezes lived
not far from Papá Chayo's *rancho*.
On the ground floor of their house,
a garage to sell gasoline,
a pool hall,
and a grocery store
where César sold sodas,
cigarettes, and candy.

César's *tíos* and *tías*
and his one hundred and eighty cousins
were his customers.
Business was good!

# The Depression

In the 1930s,
César's *tíos* and *tías*
—along with many other Americans—
lost their jobs.
What could Librado do but help them?
He let them have anything
they needed from the store.
They could pay him later,
when things got better.
But things didn't get better.
Before long, the store was empty.
Librado had no money to refill it
and lost the business in a bad deal.
But they still had Papá Chayo's *rancho*!

In the *rancho*,
César and his brother Richard
slept on the pool table that
Librado had not been able to sell.
"Look!" César told Richard,
pointing at the peeling plaster.
"There's a face over there.
And look in the corner, here's a rabbit!"

# Papá Chayo's Rancho

César tried selling eggs,
leaving home
with a basket of eggs,
returning with a loaf of bread.

When Vicky was born,
Librado paid the doctor
with watermelons.

To earn money
to keep Papá Chayo's *rancho*,
Librado left home
to work as a farm worker.
Soon his family joined him
in the California fields.

César and Richard made balls
out of tinfoil and sold them.
They swept out a movie theater
where they saw *The Lone Ranger*.
They also worked hard *piscando*
walnuts, peas, apricots.

Still, the Chávezes lost
Papá Chayo's *rancho*.

"A red tractor came to the farm.
Its motor blotted out
the sound of crickets and bullfrogs
and the buzzing of the flies.
It destroyed the trees,
pushing them to the side
as if they were nothing.
My dad would never let us
carve our initials or do anything to those trees."

# On the Move

They followed the crops.
"Our cars loaded with mattresses,
baggage, and kids told
everyone a familiar story."
Stopping wherever ripeness hung.

They stayed
in a broken-down shed.
No doors.
A dirty toilet outdoors.
They drank and bathed in ditches.
Talk of an illness in the camp
made them move out.

A *patrón* let the Chávezes
stay in a house
that had hot water,
gas, electricity, two bedrooms,
and a clean toilet nearby.
The Chávezes stayed
until the trees were bare.

The following winter
they lived in a tent
set in a puddle-filled lot.
The girls, Juana, and Librado
slept in the tent.
The boys slept out,
between the wet dirt and wet sky.

# Green Gold

*Lechuguero,*
a lettuce thinner,
a man, a woman, or a child
who pulls off smaller plants
to make room for bigger plants—
the *patrón's* green gold.

Row after row,
César walked.
Stooped over, twisted,
clawing at the *chuga*
with *el cortito,*
a short-handed hoe.

No boots, just shoes
sinking in mud,
clay clinging to the soles.

Every day swathed in scarves
covering his nose and mouth.
Trying not to breathe,
trying not to swallow
the smelly spray blowing on him.

Armpits sweating,
back aching . . . aching . . . aching.
Too tired to feel the hunger.

# I Am a Clown

One word in Spanish,
just one word,
and *¡Fuii!* whistled the ruler
across César's knuckles,
its edge cutting sharply.

The teacher hung a sign
around his neck:
"I am a clown.
I speak Spanish."

"If you're an American,"
she said,
"speak only in English.
If you want to speak in Spanish,
go back to Mexico."

At home a *dicho*:
*"Quien sabe dos lenguas vale por dos."*
He who knows two languages
is more valuable than he who knows only one.

Mother told César,
"I didn't learn,
but you can learn,
so you have to go to school."

Even if they were in a place
for a day or two,
Mother made him go.
César went to more than thirty schools.

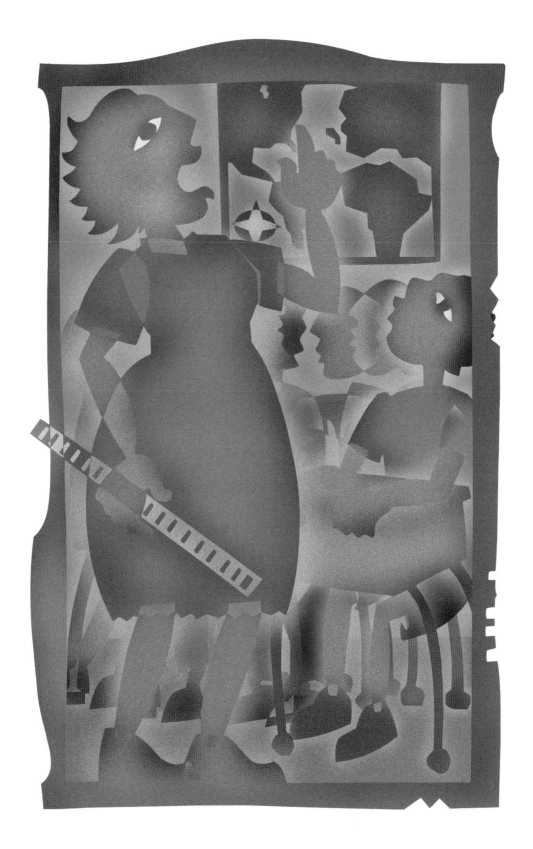

# Prayer of the Farm Workers' Struggle

"Give me honesty and patience;
so that I can work with other workers."

At five in the morning,
a *raitero* with a *troca*
picked them up.
Twenty-five cents a ride
each would have to pay,
more sometimes
than they made in a day.

A *contratista* found them work
*piscando* peas for good wages!
They got paid half
of the promised pay—late.

Twelve cents an hour
for thinning cantaloupes.
The *mayordomo* paid César
eight cents an hour.
But he'd thinned as much as the others!
Ah! But he was eleven, short, and thin.

*Raiteros, contratistas, mayordomos,*
most Mexicans or Mexican-Americans,
trying to make a living in an ugly way.

"Help us love even those who hate us;
so we can change the world."

# Pachuco Days

"From now on, Mother," César said
after his eighth-grade graduation,
"you're not going to step one foot
out of the house to work anymore!"
Juana's heart broke at his words.
No more school for César.

He worked in the fields
until the day he yelled,
"Dad, I've had it!"
and joined the navy.

When he returned,
the country had jobs!
A steady job, please.
A job with a future—
for the future's children.

No jobs for him but in the fields.
For this Mexican-American,
school-dropout *pachuco* wearing
thick soles, pegged pants, long coats,
only a job in the fields!

# Vírgen de Guadalupe

"I decided to challenge the theater's rule.
Instead of sitting on the right,
I sat down on the left.
When I was asked to move,
I refused.
The police took me to jail."
(*Duele, Vírgen de Guadalupe,*
discrimination hurts deeply.)

"I went to this little malt shop, *La Baratita.*
That's where I saw Helen for the first time.
I remember she had flowers in her hair."
(*No sé lo que valga mi vida, Vírgen de Guadalupe,*
I don't know if my life is worth anything,
but I will share it with her.)

"We had a one-room shack
in the San Jose barrio
of Sal Si Puedes."
(*Sal Si Puedes, Vírgen de Guadalupe,*
Get Out If You Can!)

"Bitterly cold
with only a kerosene camping stove
kept on day and night."
(*Cobijas, Vírgen de Guadalupe,*
warm blankets for our children!)

"When we stepped out,
we stepped out right into the mud—
thick, black clay."
(*Un patio verde, Vírgen de Guadalupe,*
a green yard for our children!)

"What a terrible irony it is
that the very people
who harvest the food we eat
do not have enough food
for their own children."
(*Frijoles, Vírgen de Guadalupe,*
a bit of beans for our children!)

# Crooked Lines

"God writes in exceedingly
crooked lines."

What made César follow
Father McDonnell
from camp to camp
and Mass to Mass?

What made Father McDonnell
give César the teachings and prayers
of Saint Francis of Assisi:
"Lord, make me an instrument
of your peace"?

Why did a book about Saint Francis
mention Mahatma Gandhi,
a man of peace who won many battles
against injustices in India?

Why did César talk
to Father McDonnell
about his passion for peaceful change
and the leadership hidden deep
inside him?

What made Father McDonnell
send Fred Ross, from the
Community Service Organization,
to see César?

God's crooked lines.

# Learning What Was Inside of Him

César crossed the street
to his brother Richard's house
and watched as a *gringo*
parked his beat-up car.
Out came a lanky guy,
his clothes wrinkled.

Fred Ross was his name.
He kept coming back,
but César would not see him.
"Well," said Helen,
"this time you tell him."

Finally César met him.
"Fred did such a good job
of explaining how poor people
could build power
that I could even taste it.
I could feel it."

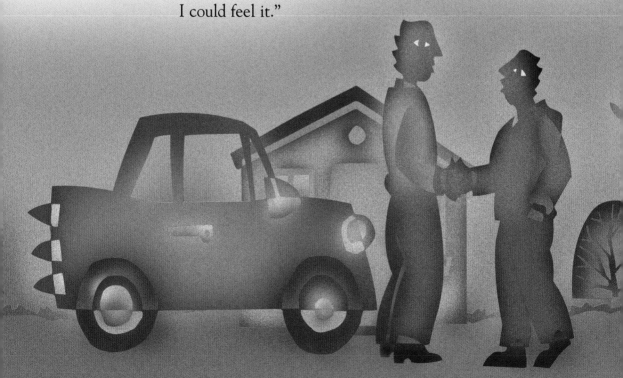

That same night,
César went to work for Ross
in the Community Service Organization.
"You don't have to parrot me
to learn to organize," Ross told him.
"Just be yourself."

Little by little,
house by house,
community by community,
city by city,
year after year,
César gave speeches
persuading Mexican-Americans to vote.

He had a good salary.
But the *campesinos* didn't.
"I resign," he told Fred one day.
César would go back to the fields
to organize a union for farm workers.
"I didn't know if I would succeed,
but I had to try."

# Delano

To Delano,
César, Helen,
and their eight children moved.

To Delano,
where the vineyards
were glossy green in the spring.

To Delano,
where at the *pisca*
the *viñeros*
were scarlet and golden brown
like *campesino* skin.

To Delano,
where there was farm work
all year long
for Helen, who was willing
to stick it out as long as it took,
and where César Chávez
could dig ditches on Sundays
to earn money to feed his *chavalos*.

To Delano,
where *campesinos* with scarred hands
came and stayed.
César began to organize not just a union
but *La Causa*, a body of peaceful people
who would ask for better pay,
better housing,
better health.
"To satisfy the farm workers' hunger
for decency and dignity and self-respect."

# Don't Mourn—Organize!

"If you don't read new books,
you are left behind.
I spend time reading into the night.
I want to be ahead of others."

With only three hours of sleep,
César left his $50 rent-per-month house,
passed the many small green houses
planted in the dust,
and beat the dawn on the long walk
to his Forty-Acres office.

He sat at his red Formica desk,
built by his brother Richard.
Organizers Dolores Huerta,
Richard, and cousin Manuel came in.
Butcher paper hung on the wall
with an agenda.
Peaceful strikes? Peaceful marches?
"You're crazy!" they said.
"It can't be done!"
"There is a way.
You just haven't figured it out yet.
Come back when you have."

To the fields César went,
where *campesinos* mourned.
"It is true that you have awful wages
and poor living and working conditions.
It is your fault.
You let them do it.
And only you can change
what is happening to you.
You—we—have that power.
Each of us has the power
to control our lives.
When we take that power,
we can improve our living
and working conditions."

The *campesinos* proved
they had *sangre brava y colorada*,
blood as red as that of other human beings.
Brave blood!
They joined the United Farm Workers union.

# ¡Sí, se puede!
# Yes, We Can!

How did César do it?
Asking farm workers to walk out of their jobs.
*¡Huelga!* Strike!
*¡Viva La Causa!* Long live The Cause
for freedom, dignity, and respect!

How did César do it?
Leading a 300-mile *peregrinación*
of *campesinos*
from Delano to Sacramento.
Limping on blistered feet,
the Aztec eagle on their union flag flying.

How did César do it?
Not eating at times.
A "Fast for Love"
to draw attention to nonviolence.
A "Fast for Life"
to draw the attention of the world
to *campesinos* with breathing difficulties,
*campesinos* with skin rashes,
*campesinos* dying of cancer
because of pesticides
that the government insisted
did no harm.

How did César do it?
Asking people to boycott
grapes and lettuce
until the pesticides were banned,
until the *campesinos*
could get better ways to live,
ways . . . to live.

Much good came out of it.
"Farm workers are struggling out
of their poverty and powerlessness."

"*¡Sí, se puede!* Yes, we can!"
"The answer lies with you and me."

# More Time Than Life

"'*Hay más tiempo que vida.*
There is more time than life.'
That is one of our *dichos*.
We don't worry about time,
because time and history are on our side."

Cesario Estrada Chávez
died in his sleep on April 23, 1993,
in San Luis, Arizona—
near the Yuma of his birth,
the Yuma of Papá Chayo's *rancho*.

Because of César Chávez
and the sacrifices of *La Causa*,
the short-handled hoe was banned
and most *campesinos* got better wages,
field toilets, rest periods, cold drinking water,
unemployment benefits, pensions, medical coverage.

Because of César Chávez
and the courage of *La Causa*,
growers provide protective masks and gloves,
consumers are more aware of the food they buy,
DDT and other pesticides have been banned,
and some people are more gentle with the earth.

Because of César Chávez
and the nonviolent empowerment of *La Causa*,
most *campesinos* now are treated with dignity
and have won back their self-respect.

At the time of his death,
César Chávez owned no car.
He'd never owned a house.

"True wealth is not measured in money
or status or power.
It is measured in the legacy we leave behind
for those we love and those we inspire."

# Notes

**Dedication**
"champion *La Raza*": McGregor, *Remembering Cesar*, p. 72.
**Dad: Librado Chávez**
"Never afraid of work": Levy, *Cesar Chavez*, p. 8.
"But if somebody was fired": Ibid., p. 33.
**Mom: Juana Estrada**
"Her tongue skipping": Levy, *Cesar Chavez*, p. 8.
"What does the Lord": Jensen and Hammerback, *The Words of César Chávez*, p. 173.
"God gave you": Levy, *Cesar Chavez*, p. 18.
**Happy Moments**
"I had more happy moments": California Curriculum Project, "César E. Chávez's Biography."
"There was an endless droning": Levy, *Cesar Chavez*, p. 10.
**The Depression**
"Look! There's a face": Levy, *Cesar Chavez*, p. 11.
**Papá Chayo's *Rancho***
"A red tractor came": Levy, *Cesar Chavez*, p. 41.
**On the Move**
"Our cars loaded": Levy, *Cesar Chavez*, p. 51.
**I Am a Clown**
"I am a clown": Taylor, *Chavez and the Farm Workers*, p. 64.
"If you're an American": Paraphrase, Levy, *Cesar Chavez*, p. 24.
"I didn't learn": Ibid., p. 65.
**Prayer of the Farm Workers' Struggle**
"Give me honesty": Chávez, *Prayer of the Farm Workers' Struggle*, www.salsa.net/peace/pray4.html
"Help us love": Ibid.
***Pachuco* Days**
"From now on": Levy. *Cesar Chavez*, p. 72.
"Dad, I've had it!": Collins, *Farmworker's Friend*, p. 20.
***Vírgen de Guadalupe***
"I decided to challenge": Levy, *Cesar Chavez*, p. 86.
"I went to this little malt shop": Ibid.
"*No sé lo que valga*": From the mariachi song "Paloma Querida."
"We had a one-room shack:" Levy, *Cesar Chavez*, p. 87.
"Bitterly cold": Paraphrase, Ibid.
"When we stepped out": Paraphrase, Ibid.
"What a terrible irony": Jensen and Hammerback, *The Words of César Chávez*, p. 167.
**Crooked Lines**
"God writes": Levy, *Cesar Chavez*, p. 42.

**Learning What Was Inside of Him**
"Well, this time you tell him":  Matthiessen, *Sal Si Puedes*, p. 44.
"Fred did such a good job": Levy, *Cesar Chavez*, p. 99.
"You don't have to parrot me": Jensen and Hammerback, *The Words of César Chávez*, p. 174.
"I resign": Levy, *Cesar Chavez*, p. 147.
"I didn't know if I would succeed": Jensen and Hammerback, *The Words of César Chávez*, p. 123.
**Delano**
"To satisfy": Jensen and Hammerback, *The Words of César Chávez*, p. 38.
**Don't Mourn—Organize!**
"If you don't read": McGregor, *Remembering Cesar*, p. 40.
"You're crazy!": Levy, *Cesar Chavez*, p. 164.
"It can't be done": McGregor, *Remembering Cesar*, p. 30.
"There is a way:" Ibid.
"It is true":  Ibid., p. 68.
"*Sangre brava*": From the mariachi song "Tequila con Limón."
**¡Sí, se puede!**
"Farm workers are struggling out": Jensen and Hammerback, *The Words of César Chávez*, p. 64.
"¡Sí, se puede!": McGregor, *Remembering Cesar*, p. 5.
"The answer lies": Ibid, p.12.
**More Time Than Life**
"*Hay más tiempo*": Matthiessen, *Sal Si Puedes*, p. 35.
"True wealth": Jensen and Hammerback, *The Words of César Chávez*, p. 98.
**¡Viva La Causa!**
"Cut the nonsense": Matthiessen, *Sal Si Puedes*, p. 115.
"If you look back": "Viva La Causa," César Chávez interviewed by Wendy Goepel.
**Chronology**
"One of the heroic figures": Internet: www.clnet.ucr.edu

# Glossary

*Abuelito*: Grandfather

*Barrio*: Slang for a neighborhood that is a slum

*Campesinos*: Farm workers

*La Causa*: The Cause, a peaceful labor-union and civil-rights movement built around the idea that people must do things by themselves to help themselves

*Chavalos*: Children

*Chuga*: Short for *lechuga*, lettuce

*Cobijas*: Blankets

*Como un guitarrón*: Like a *guitarrón*; a *guitarrón* is a large instrument that has six strings plucked in pairs, which makes the bass part louder.

*Como una vihuela*: Like a *vihuela*; a *vihuela* is a small instrument that has five strings that are plucked, making a crisp, clear sound.

*Contratista*: Contractor; a person who found jobs for the farm workers

*El cortito*: A short-handled hoe

*Dichos*: Sayings, proverbs

*Duele*: It hurts.

*En el día de su santo*: On his birth date

*Frijoles*: Beans

*¡Fuii!*: Sound that the ruler made

*La gente*: The people

*El Gringo*: Slang for "American"

*Hay más tiempo que vida.*: There is more time than life.

*¡Híjole!*: Wow!

*¡Huelga!*: Strike!

*Lechuguero*: Lettuce thinner

*Manzanilla*: Chamomile. César drank so much *manzanilla* that the family called him Manzi.

*Mayordomo*: Overseer, boss

*No sé lo que valga mi vida*: I don't know if my life is worth anything.

*Pachuco*: A teenager who rebels against his Mexican roots. As an adolescent, César liked to dance the boogie-woogie but hated mariachi music and his mother's *manzanilla* tea.

*Pan dulce*: Mexican sweet bread

*Patio verde*: Green yard

*Patrón*: Grower, boss

*Peregrinación*: Pilgrimage

*Pisca*: Harvest

*Piscando*: A word farm workers use for picking fruit and vegetables at harvesttime.

*Quien sabe dos lenguas vale por dos*: He who knows two languages is more valuable than he who knows only one.

*Raitero*: Slang for drivers who gave rides to farm workers

*Rancho*: Ranch

*La Raza*: The Race. Because Latinos are of mixed races, some Hispanics use this term to describe themselves. César cared for people beyond *La Raza*. He cared for *la raza humana*.

*La raza humana*: The human race

*Sal Si Puedes*: A tough *barrio* in San Jose, California, named "Get Out If You Can" because people only left to go to jail, the military, or the cemetery

*Sangre brava y colorada*: Brave, red blood

*¡Sí, se puede!*: "Yes, We Can!" was César's motto.

*Tías/Tíos*: Aunts/uncles

*Troca*: Slang for "truck." The correct word in Spanish is *camión*.

*Viñeros*: Vineyards

*Vírgen de Guadalupe*: Patron saint of Mexico who appeared in a vision to Juan Diego, a Mexican Indian in Guadalupe

*¡Viva La Causa!*: Long live The Cause!

# ¡Viva La Causa!
# Long Live The Cause!:
# César's Life Story

César Estrada Chávez was born near Yuma, Arizona, on March 31, 1927. He had four siblings: Rita, Richard (Rukie), Eduvigis (Vicky), and Librado (Lenny). Cousin Manuel Chávez also lived with them. They called César Manzi because he drank a lot of *manzanilla* tea.

When César was ten years old, he moved with his family to California, where they all became farm workers. They earned low wages and lived in shacks or wherever they could find a place to lay their heads.

There were no unions just for farm workers, but César's father held meetings for his fellow workers at his house. César listened and learned. His mother—who originally inspired her son's nonviolent approach—didn't like the unions because they sometimes practiced violent means to achieve change. When the Chávez family witnessed an injustice, they would protest by walking off the field.

The Chávezes moved a lot as they followed the crops. César attended more than thirty schools. He graduated from eighth grade but then dropped out to help support the family by continuing to work in the fields.

In 1946 César joined the navy and served as a deckhand in the western Pacific. When he returned, he married Helen Fabela. They eventually had eight children: Eloise, Fernando (Polly), Paul (Babo), Linda, Sylvia (Mia), Anthony (Birdy), Elizabeth (Liz), and Anna.

In 1952 César met Fred Ross, an organizer for the Community Service Organization. Suspicious of Ross's motives at first, César eventually joined Ross to help Latinos become citizens. They also registered them to vote. In 1956 César became the organization's general director.

In 1962 César quit his job and moved to Delano, California, to organize, with colleague Dolores Huerta, the first union for farm workers. The National Farm Worker Association—later the United

Farm Workers (UFW)—was not just a union but *La Causa*, a civil-rights movement that empowered farm workers to change their own working conditions and improve the quality of their lives.

When a group of Filipino farm workers went on strike, César and the other UFW members joined them on the picket lines. The union opened membership to the Filipinos, and all the members committed themselves to bringing about change through nonviolent means.

In 1966 Chávez—inspired by Dr. Martin Luther King Jr.—organized a march from Delano to Sacramento that won the UFW more than ten thousand supporters. In 1977 he settled a five-year battle with the Teamsters, a transportation union organizing farm workers in competition with the UFW. César also conducted fasts to support the union's pledge of nonviolence and to draw the world's attention to the use of pesticides in the fields. His worldwide boycotts caused grape sales to fall to such a low point that the growers had to negotiate with the UFW for better wages, improved working conditions, and reduced use of pesticides.

Because of César's accomplishments, some people thought he was a saint. To that he said, "Cut the nonsense." He was human, not superhuman.

Around 9:00 AM on Friday, April 23, 1993, a UFW officer found César still in bed—clothes on, no shoes, and a book about Native Americans by his side. César had died in his sleep.

More than 40,000 people attended his funeral in Delano. He was buried at the foot of the hill that he often climbed to watch the sunrise in La Paz, California.

César Chávez has not been forgotten. California, New Mexico, Texas, Colorado, and Arizona have declared March 31 César Chávez Day. In California, it's a paid holiday. Many schools and centers are named after him, and students continue to learn about *La Causa*. In 2003, the United States Post Office issued a César Chávez commemorative stamp.

Today the UFW has more than 100,000 members, and offices in California, Texas, Arizona, and Florida. Some states, however, are trying to pass laws against the rights of farm workers to strike and boycott. It is as César once said, "If you look back, we have come a long way; if you look ahead, we have a long way to go."

But César Chávez proved his motto: ¡*Sí, se puede!*

# Chronology

1927—On March 31, Cesario Estrada Chávez is born near Yuma, Arizona.

1934—Cesario starts going to school, where his name becomes César.

1937—Librado Chávez moves to California, and his family later follows him.

1942—César graduates from eighth grade and drops out of school to work in the fields.

1944—César breaks the rules in a movie theater by refusing to sit in the section for Mexicans; he spends an hour in jail.

1946—César enlists in the United States Navy.

1948—César is discharged from the navy and marries Helen Fabela.

1952—César helps Father Donald McDonnell, meets Fred Ross, and works with Ross for the Community Service Organization (CSO).

1956—César becomes a general director of the CSO.

1962—César resigns from the CSO and moves to Delano to start the National Farm Workers Association, later the United Farm Workers of America (UFW).

1965—On September 8, Filipino grape pickers in Delano go on strike for higher wages. The National Farm Workers Association joins the strike.

1966—César leads a march from Delano to Sacramento.

1967—The grape boycott begins.

1968—On February 14, César begins a twenty-five-day fast in favor of nonviolence. Senator Robert F. Kennedy describes him as "one of the heroic figures of our times." On March 24, a nationwide boycott of California grapes begins.

1969—On May 10, an international grape boycott is declared.

1970—Contract agreements are reached between the UFW and major grape growers. Grape boycotts and strikes end. The Teamsters Union signs contracts with growers to keep the UFW out of the fields. A boycott of lettuce starts.

1972—César fasts from May 11 to June 4 to protest an Arizona law that prevents workers from striking or boycotting.

1973—New boycotts begin when grape growers fail to renew their contracts.

1975—César helps California governor Jerry Brown pass the California Agricultural Labor Relations Act, giving farm workers the right to have a union.

1977—The Teamsters Union agrees to leave the fields to the UFW.

1979—The UFW wins its demand for a significant pay raise.

1982—Governor George Deukmejian vetoes bills in favor of farm workers.

1984—In January, César calls for another grape boycott.

1988—César fasts for thirty-six days, a "Fast for Life."

1992—Grape workers get their first pay raise in nine years.

1993—On April 23, César dies in his sleep in San Luis, Arizona, only a few miles from his birthplace. On April 29, forty thousand mourners attend his funeral in Delano.

1994—The Cesar E. Chavez Foundation is established to promote the ideals, work, and vision of La Causa. President William J. Clinton presents the Medal of Freedom to César Chávez. Helen accepts the medal in a special ceremony at the White House on August 8.

# Sources

## Web Sites

California Curriculum Project, *Hispanic Biographies*, "César E. Chávez's Biography," 1994. Internet: www.sfsu.edu

César E. Chávez, "One of the Heroic Figures of Our Time," 1927-1993. Internet: www.clnet.ucr.edu

César Chávez, "Prayer of the Farm Workers' Struggle." Internet: http://www.salsa.net/peace/pray4.html

Cesar E. Chavez Foundation. Los Angeles. Internet: www.cesarechavezfoundation.org

United Farm Workers. Los Angeles. Internet: www.ufw.org

## Publications and Interviews

**Altman, Linda Jacobs.** *The Importance of Cesar Chavez*. San Diego: Lucent Books, 1996. **Ayala, Rudolfo,** and **Gaspar Enriquez** (illustrator). *Elegy on the Death of César Chávez*. El Paso: Cinco Puntos Press, 2000. **Bernier-Grand, Carmen T.** Interview with Dolores Huerta. César E. Chávez Leadership Conference. Portland, Oregon, March 10, 2003. **Bernier-Grand, Carmen T.** Online fact exchange with Julie C. Rodríguez, Cesar E. Chavez Foundation Community Programs Office, July 11, 2003. **Collins, David R.** *Farmworker's Friend: The Story of Cesar Chavez*. Minneapolis: Carolrhoda Books, Inc., 1996. **Day, Mark.** *Forty Acres: Cesar Chavez and the Farm Workers*. New York: Praeger Publishers, 1971. **Dunne, John Gregory.** *Delano: The Story of the California Grape Strike*. New York: Farrar, Straus & Giroux, 1967. **Ferriss, Susan,** and **Ricardo Sandoval.** *The Fight in the Fields: Cesar Chavez and the Farmworkers Movement*. New York: Harcourt Brace, 1997. **Franchere, Ruth.** *Cesar Chavez*. New York: HarperCollins, 1970; sixth reprint ed. **Goepel, Wendy.** "Viva La Causa." Interview with César E. Chávez. Internet: www.sfsu.edu **Griswold, Richard Del Castillo,** and **Richard A García.** *Cesar Chavez: A Triumph of Spirit*. Norman, OK: University of Oklahoma Press, 1995. Interview with César Chávez. Pacífica Radio Archive. Los Angeles, 1986. **Jensen, Richard J.,** and **John C. Hammerback.** *The Words of César Chávez*. Texas: Texas A & M University Press, 2002. **Krull, Kathleen,** and **Yuyi Morales** (Illustrator). *Harvesting Hope*. San Diego: Harcourt, 2003. **Levy, Jacques.** *Cesar Chavez: Autobiography of La Causa*. New York: W.W. Norton, 1975. **Matthiessen, Peter.** *Sal Si Puedes (Escape If You Can): Cesar Chavez and the New American Revolution*. Berkeley: University of California Press, 1969. **McGregor, Ann.** *Remembering Cesar: The Legacy of Cesar Chavez*. Clovis, CA: Quill Driver Books/Word Dancer Press, 2000. **Orr, Kathy** and **Louise Mehler.** *Health and Safety Report*. "Physician Reporting of Pesticide Illness." March 20, 2000. **Pérez, Frank.** *Dolores Huerta*. Austin: Raintree/Steck-Vaughn, 1996. **Taylor, Ronald.** *Chavez and the Farm Workers*. Boston: Beacon Press, 1975. **United States General Accounting Office Report to Congressional Requesters.** "Pesticides: Improvement Needed to Ensure the Safety of Farmworkers and Their Children," March 2000.

# In His Own Words

"Once social change begins, it cannot be reversed. You cannot uneducate the person who has learned to read. You cannot humiliate the person who feels pride. You cannot oppress the people who are not afraid anymore." UFW's Seventh Constitutional Convention, September 1984. Internet: www.ufw.org

"Anyone who comes in with the idea that farmworkers are free of sin and that growers are all bastards either has never dealt with the situation or is an idealist of the first order." Ferriss and Sandoval, *The Fight in the Fields*, p. 64.

"My dream is that farm workers will someday have enough power to take care of themselves, and if they gain that, that they don't become selfish . . ." La Paz, California, October 1971. Jensen and Hammerback, *The Words of César Chávez*, p. 71.

"Violence does not work in the long run and if it is temporarily successful, it replaces one violent form of power with another just as violent." Jensen and Hammerback, *The Words of César Chávez*, p. 97.

"You can't fool Mother Nature . . . using pesticides that kill off their natural predators . . . at what cost? The lives of the farm workers and children who are suffering? The lives of consumers who could reap the harvest of pesticides ten, twenty years from now? The contamination of our ground water? The loss of our reverence for the soil? The raping of the land? People forget that the soil is our sustenance. It is a sacred trust. It is what has worked for us for centuries. It is what we pass on to future generations." Speech at Pacific Lutheran University, March 1989. Jensen and Hammerback, *The Words of César Chávez*, p. 149.

"All around us were those who said that it could never be done. Everywhere people said that the growers were too strong for us, that the police would be against us, that the courts would beat us down, and that sooner or later we would fall back into the poverty of our forefathers. But we fooled them. We fooled them because our common suffering and our love for each other and our families kept us together sacrificing and fighting for the better tomorrow . . ." Speech in Coachella, 1973. Jensen and Hammerback, *The Words of César Chávez*, p. 78.